W9-BVI-354

Madness

Harcourt Brace Jovanovich

New York and London

Hamburger

Cartoons by Jack Ziegler

Preface by Brian McConnachie

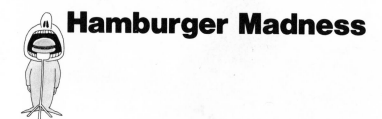# Hamburger Madness

To Madam

Copyright © 1978 by Jack Ziegler

All rights reserved. No part of this publication may be reproduced or transmitted in any form or by any means, electronic or mechanical, including photocopy, recording, or any information storage and retrieval system, without permission in writing from the publisher.

The author wishes to thank these publications for permission to reprint cartoons on the pages given: *Esquire*, 18 (bottom), 104, 114, © 1976 by Esquire, Inc., and 64, © 1977 by Esquire Magazine Inc.; *Medical Economics*, 58 (bottom), © 1976 by Medical Economics Magazine; *National Lampoon,* 102, © 1975 by National Lampoon, Inc.; *The New Yorker*, 11, 12, 13 (top), 19, 20, 22, 24 (top), 25, 26 (top), 31–33, 35 (top), 36 (top), 37, 40, 43 (top), 46, 47 (top), 48, 55, 57 (top), 60 (bottom), 61, 62, 67, 68 (top), 72, 74 (bottom), 75–78, 81 (top), 83, 84 (top), 85, 86, 89, 91, 93 (top), 94, 97, 100, 103, 106, 108, 111 (bottom), 113, 115 (top), 116, 117, 125, copyright © 1974, 1975, 1976, 1977 by The New Yorker Magazine, Inc.; *The New York Times*, 59, © 1977 by The New York Times Company; *Writer's Digest*, 34, copyright © 1975 by *Writer's Digest*; *Writer's Yearbook*, 128, copyright © 1975 by *Writer's Yearbook.*

Printed in the United States of America

Library of Congress Cataloging in Publication Data
Ziegler, Jack.
      Hamburger madness.

      1.   American wit and humor, Pictorial.   I.   Title.
NC1429.Z47A4   1978   973.926′02′07   78-53915
ISBN 0-15-138417-7

First edition
B C D E

Preface

Jack Ziegler sat on a San Francisco beach and watched his dog chase, then flee, the breaking waves. With him on that chilly May afternoon were his wife and a few friends all sharing a picnic. His face, buffeted by the sea wind, was a reddish petal budding through dark, wintry hair. With his back erect and his gaze fixed to the distance, he had the look of a visionary resigned to suffer the elements in order to understand them.

The picnic guests were discussing deranged arsonists.

"No . . . no . . . first you lock them up, *then* you treat them."

"Fine. But what do you do when they turn around and burn the place down?"

"Yes, then all of the other deranged people escape."

"Which is better: one guilty arsonist roaming free or hundreds of guilty madmen running wild?"

Jack kept out of the conversation. He was the only one there who actually knew an arsonist: a fellow he had met in the Army whose plan was to burn it down. All he could ever get to catch on fire, however, was the mail in the mailroom and his own bed. Jack leaned forward for a peek into the picnic basket. With one finger, he pushed aside and separated the various eats. At the very bottom was a package wrapped in cellophane and labeled Jams of Tiny Enslaved Nations. Jellies and preserves, jams and marmalades, clustered together in a brave little salute to the peoples of the world who have rejected oppression as an unprincipled way of life. His visionary look turned to one of curiosity as he read the contents from the jar tops: Bilberry, Caprifig, Pond Apple, Mombin, Muskmelon, Whortleberry, Acorn, Cytoglobin. He removed the cap from a Latvian Jackfruit Jam with Pits and took a whiff. What little fragrance there was smelled like lima beans.

"Put them in fireproof cells."

"Wait a minute. . . . Why the hell should the other maniacs be forced into fireproof cells just because . . . ?"

"You don't tell them, for God's sake. What do you think—some orderly is going to walk in and say, 'Excuse me, Napoleon, you want to gather up your feces collection, you're going to have to move. It's nothing personal, mind you. . . .'"

"I don't agree. Why should we have to reorder our system because of them?"

The lima-bean smell brought Jack back to the early Sixties and to the East Coast, where he had lived. Those great walloping pots of lima beans they were always cooking up at the once grand Forest Hills Inn (Jack's in-

74834

between-rounds hangout) where it was more action than laughter and more laughter than talk: the original "kissing bandit" convention hall. And Jack, the first Champagne Twin: fast-dealing, finger-snapping, trouble-ducking, head-tossing, wise-cracking, belly-scratching, trend-setting, high-rolling cock-o'-the-walk. He started adding "ie" to the end of everybody's last name, and *everybody* started adding "ie" to the end of everybody's last name. He introduced the palm-to-palm chimpanzee style of applause, replacing the fingers-to-palm conventional style because ". . . we're livin' a monkey kind of life." When the crowds and the sport got a little too unwieldy upstairs, there was a downstairs to retreat to. A double-decker fun bin. The Forest Hills Inn was that kind of place. Old man Stein, the downstairs maitre d', would wave a signal to the room if he saw Jack descending. "Hi, Steinie, how'm I doin'?" "I'll tell you this—you're young, but you're no cheese-face kid." Jack would usually slip him a fiver but warn him with a wink that the ink was still wet. "Don't spend it all on lima beans."

If the other Champagne Twin was perched by the piano, there'd be a game, a contest called "Answer the Questions." The piano player did the asking. General information questions like: what's the water content of a banana? Once in a while, he'd get to use his piano and would sing the question. First prize for a complete and correct answer sheet was a bottle of champagne. No one stood a chance against the Twins. But others played just to watch them operate and to say that they were once in the battle. The Twins' style of play was a style they called Nellie-Bar-the-Door. A strictly no-holds-barred, anything-goes, answer-the-questions-or-be-damned style. They copied from others, they bit people on the wrist, they dragged people out of the room, they rejected questions, they threw beer mugs, they ordered the rules changed, they grabbed women by the hair and spun them around—anything they had to do to win, and win they always did. It was a wonder to see what extremes they would take to snatch victory. But when they got their champagne, they always shared it and meekly asked to be forgiven for the disgraceful things they had just done. They would say, "But you must understand what winning means to us or there is absolutely no sense in playing this kooky game," and offer other wordy reasons for carrying on as they did. But everyone knew it was just the champagne they were after. They chugged it from the bottle, exchanging grins as they wiped away the excess bubbles from their lips. They were always forgiven. The Forest Hills Inn was the kind of hangout where grace always trumped revenge so that tomorrow would be more fun than today.

But tomorrow finally came to an end with a rhythm too fast and a beat too independent for the strangers who could have inherited and maintained the pace. Maybe the fun was top-heavy. Maybe the antics were too threatening or maybe it was the bubble-gum quiche that Jack put on their menu. It ended with the slam of a steel gate across the interior entrance to the upstairs bar.

People still lived in the rooms above, and Jack dropped by one day to visit. He paused at the gate for a last look in and saw Swampy, an old habitué, on the floor, tucked in a corner. Cats wandered about, brushing against empty bottles, spinning them in their wake. It was a ghost town in there. Swampy's knees, drawn up to his chin, were capped with sooty, rubber novelty bosoms between which his chin rested. "Hey, Swampy, whatcha doin' in there?" There was no sign of recognition. "It's all shut down, Swamps, come on out of there." Swampy took the bosoms and put them over his eyes and rolled his head from side to side, looking like some spoiled-brat space bug defying parental authority. He dropped his legs to the floor and slid away from the wall to lie on his back. The kitties tiptoed over, whiffing as they went, to see if Swampy was still a good source of heat. Jack realized the Swampy was in there for good and wondered if anyone would even go in there for the body. It was going to be all those cats sitting on his chest while he was still warm and then caving him in.

Shortly afterwards, Jack put his affairs in order and left for California.

"Just keep them all in strait jackets and sort of wet down everything around them."

"Fine, just fine, and suffer the consequences of turning them into raving lunatics."

"Well, they're not exactly poster candidates for Mental Health Week."

"They'd burn down Mental Health Week, given enough paper."

"What about deporting them somewhere?"

Jack stood up and walked toward the shore. He thought about moving back East. Maybe things had loosened up and he could find some kind of work.

Brian McConnachie

Winter, 1978, New York City

"It just stands there. Doesn't move! Doesn't talk! Doesn't eat!! It's driving me nuts!"

$2 PIANO

Executive Sneak Attack

MADE IN HEAVEN?

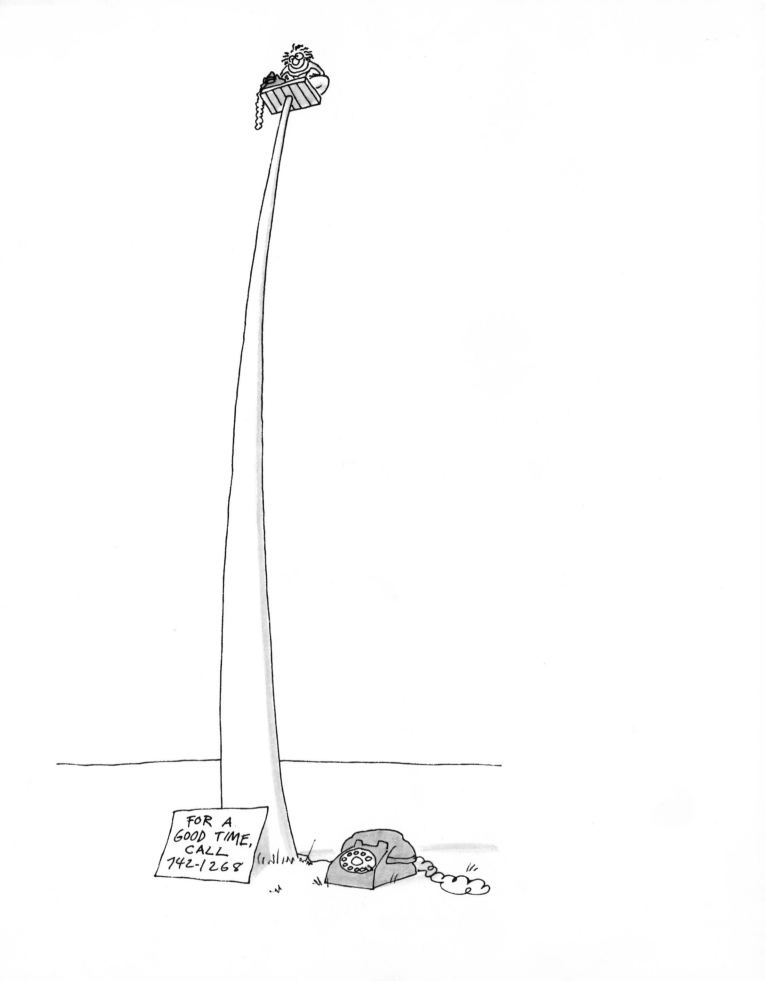

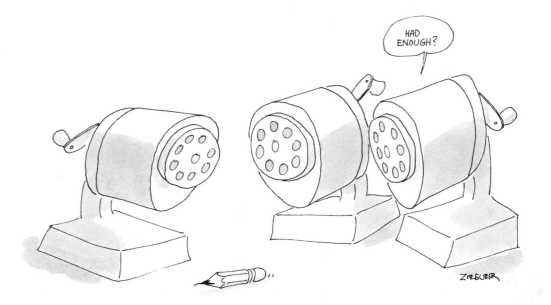

"Mine's last words were: 'Sez who?' Of course, that was back
in 1948, when talk was quite cheap."

"No, no, no, no, no, no, no, no, no, no!"

"How many times do I have to tell you, Jocelyn, 'I won't dance! Why should I? I won't dance! How could I? I won't dance! Merci beaucoup!' "

"Mornin', Mister Coffee! Up already?"

"I found myself in a small room. Soundlessly the doors slid shut after me and a sequential series of numbers on the wall began to light up - one after another. Some sort of countdown, I figured, or perhaps a trick. I became aware of a faint whirring sound and got the weird feeling I was being taken for a ride. Yet I was standing still! A fist tightened inside my stomach and I felt sick. My ears began to pop like cheap gum. Pop! Pop pop pop! This case was beginning to take on bizarre proportions, all right."

"Hi. Hildy Huffaker here with another Happy Hint for the Harried Housewife. 'A stitch in time saves nine.' Well, that's it. Bye till next time."

HEY HEY HEY, IT'S...

"And dentistry? I've heard dentistry has its rewards also."

PINOCCHIO REMINISCES ON THE LUSTY DAYS OF HIS YOUTH....

An unpleasant surprise.

THE ORIGINAL SOUNDTRACK

PLINK A-PLINK A-PLINK A-PLINK
DEEDLY-DEE DE-DEE...

PLINK A-PLINK —BAAAAA-
DAAAAAAA...

BOM BOM BOMMM BOM BOMMMMMMM...

BAM CHUNKA BAM CHUNKA BAM CHUNKA BAM CHUNKA...

SCREEEEEEEEEEE DOM DOM DOM BOOOOOOOOOOOM
THUM THUM BABOOOOOOM...

OOOO - OO - OOOOOOO - OO - WA - WA - WOOOOOOOOO...

EEEEEEEEEEEEEEEEEEEE
EEEEEEEEEEEEEE...

PLINK A-PLINK A-PLINK A-PLINK
DEEDLY-DEE DE-DEE...

"Two Cagneys and a side of Garbo to go. Hold the Bogart."

"My boy Kong, he'll be tall and as tough as a tree, will Kong,
Like a tree he'll grow with his head held high and his feet
planted firm on the ground,
And ya won't see nobody dare to try to boss him or toss him
around. . . ."

"Louise? Henry.
Hare Krishna
Hare Krishna
Krishna Krishna
Hare Hare
Hare Rama
Hare Rama
Rama Rama
Hare Hare
Did I leave my wallet on the bureau?"

GREAT MOMENTS FROM THE SILVER SCREEN

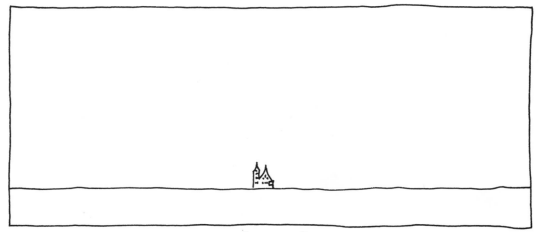

"GIANT"

"MUTINY ON THE BOUNTY"

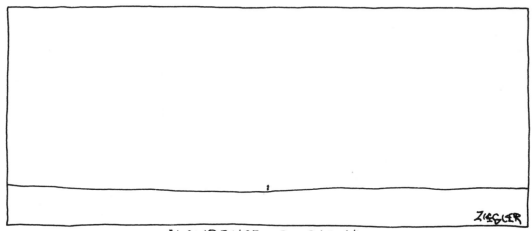

"LAWRENCE OF ARABIA"

"There I was. Peas to the left of me. Peas to the right of me.
Mashed potatoes coming down the middle. Suddenly the
hot dogs disappeared. It was now up to the celery stalks!
But could they do it without the support of the mayonnaise?"

The Miracle of Height

BEFORE WE COULD STOP HIM, UNCLE MICK HAD DRIVEN OUT OF THE PICTURE.

"Everything's under control at my end, Jenkins. Is everything under control at your end?"

"Don't bother to offer *me* any!"

"What is this—some sort of joke?"

"They tell me I'm precocious—but all I ever wanted to do
was dance."

"Mr. Carling! I know that's you! Your Nehru jacket is ready. It's *still* ready! It's been ready, Mr. Carling, for eight years now!"

A MEETING OF THE FRIARESS'S CLUB.

"More Earthlings, Bork. Pretend you're asleep."

Sand Castles

"Of course, I didn't know George was a Trekkie when I married him."

"Accepting the applause for Mr. Fontana—Mr. Fontana's
mother."

"Hello? 'Beasts of the Field'? This is Lou, over in 'Birds of the Air.' Anything funny going on at your end?"

Oct. 20, 1975

Gentlemen:
    I am not a person who generally writes letters. However, in this case, I felt that I had to.

Sincerely,
David B. Carroll

A Sudden Realization

"Is the sky blue? Is the Pope Catholic?"

"Surely not *the* Mr. Bar-B-Q!"

"Six years ago I was quite newsworthy, but nobody
followed up on it."

"What it simply comes down to, Bob, is that we're terrific 'Streetcar Named Desire' fans. I fondly call my wife Jean here Stella and she calls me Stanley. A few months after we were married we got the dog and just had to call her Blanche. We just had to. A few years after that we had the first kid and called her Jessica, after Jessica Tandy who was the original Blanche on Broadway. There followed Kim, Marlon and Elia, whose nickname is Gadge. Then the little fella came along and we decided to call him Rhett. We're pretty damned partial to 'Gone With the Wind' also."

A Potential Reject

"Now dammit, this used to be Faulkner country."

"Would you please have the orchestra play 'Tea for Two,'
and I'll just have the tea for one, thank you."

CORPORATE-SPONSORED
BIOGRAPHIES OF THE GREAT

When young Pablo arrived in Paris, he was amazed at the variety of wallpapers he had to choose from.

—"The Youth of Pablo Picasso"
© 1975, International Wallpaper Institute

Fëdor smiled grimly, knowing that the future of his hard-earned dacha, troika, and samovar depended on this next roll. He stepped forward and sent the ball on its way home.

—"Dostoevski's Luck"
© 1969, United States of America Bowling
Association

Karl glanced at the last stick of beef jerky on his plate. He longed to savor it through these final difficult paragraphs of the book that would bring him both fame and obloquy.

—"Capitalism and Lunch: The Secret Life of
Karl Marx"
© 1973, Beefy Snax Corporation

Freud lay down on the lounge chair. The gentle buzzing of the mosquitoes soon lulled him to sleep, and he dreamed a dream that would change the face of psychology forever.

—"Interpretation of Freud"
© 1958, Lawn Chairs Unlimited of Pasadena

Although Fiorello LaGuardia and Albert Einstein laughed and laughed and laughed at the joke, their socks did not fall down.

—"A Remarkable Friendship"
© 1971, He-Man Hose Manufacturing Company

Villa readjusted his sunglasses against the blazing Mexican noon and stared out across the vast expanse. "So this is it," he murmured. "The whole enchilada."

—"Pancho Villa: The Action Years"
© 1963, Sun-Ban Company

Falling Over

Inspiration

It was a Tuesday afternoon, one of those fat, sloppy, taco-flavored, lazy Los Angeles days when the heat comes seeping through the blinds like a bad memory. Motes of dust crawled through the sun's rays like snipers on a three-day binge. Suddenly a large duck appeared....

"Okay, class, what have we here? . . . Donnally? . . .
Bukowski? . . . Heilbruner? . . . Okay. It's a revolver. Now
we ask ourselves the first question. What is the first question
we ask ourselves, class? . . . Cafferata? . . . Byrne?
. . . Anybody? . . . Okay. The first question is this:
Is-it-a-clue? Right? . . . Bukowski? . . ."

Hamburger Priest

"Whose idea was this?"

"I don't know what's happening, but lately I've been feeling
afraid of my own clothes."

"Can you take it, Morrison? I like my men to be able to take it."

"... I'd walk a million miles for one of your smiles, my Maa-aaa-aaaammy. ..."

DUE NORTH OF SAN BERDOO, IN
THE MOJAVE DESERT, WHERE
THERE IS NOT MUCH ELSE TO
DO, FORMER HELL'S ANGELS
OFTEN ENTERTAIN EACH
OTHER BY IMPERSONATING
THE SUNSETS.

"There's the Secret of the Sphinx, the Mysteries of the Pyramids, the Lost Continent of Atlantis, the Bermuda Triangle, and you, Joey, you."

A LOS ANGELES BUSINESSMAN, ATTEMPTING TO REMEMBER WHAT MONTH IT IS, FINDS THAT HE IS NOT ENTIRELY CERTAIN OF THE YEAR, EITHER.

WHILE ABSORBED IN THE CEILING, GIUSEPPE TRIPPED AND FELL TO THE FLOOR OF THE SISTINE CHAPEL.

WINTER BREAKS AND SPRING BEGINS WITH SUMMER JUST AROUND THE CORNER FOR BURT IN THE AUTUMN OF HIS DAYS.

"Hello. To begin, I'd like to do my impression of a toaster. Here goes. Mmmmmmmmmmmmmmmmmmmmmmmmmmmm—

mmmmmmmmmmmmmmmmmmmm—POP! Thank you, thank you. And now, a fuse box. Ready? Mmmmmmmmmmmmmmmmm . . ."

"Hey, you! Arnold Schwarzenegger! You want to arm wrestle for shots?"

"January sixth standard salutation comma new paragraph blah blah and so forth and so on et cetera et cetera sincerely J.W.G."

DR. JONAS CAUTIONED NURSE DORSET TO STAY BEHIND WHILE HE EXPLAINED TO JANE WHAT THEY HAD FOUND IN RALPH'S STOMACH.

"Actually I'm not even a real Modo, I'm only a Quasimodo."

UNPROVOKED ASSAULTS

The Dust Ball

The Casually Tossed
Piece of Popcorn

The Surprising Jalapeño
Pepper Hors d'Oeuvre

Noon

The New Hairdo Grazing the Wind Chimes

The Inexplicable Henny Youngman
Monologue Over Muzak

"You have brought sunshine to my life and now I must say goodbye."

"I hope we've learned a little lesson here today, Jenkins."

"And to Harold I leave my briquettes, my adjustable grill,
and my hamburgers."

"Ring. Ring, you damned fiend. Ring or you will surely break my heart."

CUFF CRAZY

"Miss Higham, I believe I can squeeze in that exorcist now."

"No, I'm not Marlon Brando. But then, on the other hand, I'm
not Joe Schmo, either."

"Hey, I'm thirsty. I need a drink. A drink and a liverwurst sandwich. Hey, how about a sandwich and a beer down at Gallagher's, and then we can go shoot some pool? Or maybe take in a movie. Hey, I'm talking to you."

"I'm not wearing any pants."

"You realize, of course, Jacobi, that should anything go wrong the General and I will have to deny any knowledge of this."

"I understand that the innuendos circulating about him are rumored to be true."

LONG AFTER LOSING THE ELECTION, FRED GORT CONTINUED TO CAMPAIGN, THUS MAKING A MOCKERY OF THOSE REPORTERS WHO HAD LABELED HIM "THE I-DON'T-CARE CANDIDATE."

THE BOSS AND THE NEW
SECRETARY WHO
HAS A PH.D.

①

②

③

④

⑤

⑥

⑦

⑧

⑨

⑩

⑪

⑫

TO BE CONTINUED.....

Fish Affair

A Chance Meeting

Love at First Sight

The First Date

The Vows of Love

The Proposal

The Marriage

Honeymoon in the Bahamas

A Crisis

Children

The Golden Years

A Pipe Has...

Substance

Identity

Practicality

Wit

"And wipe that silly mustache off your face when you talk to me, Flaherty!"

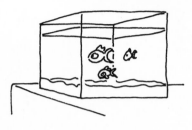

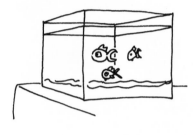

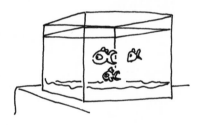

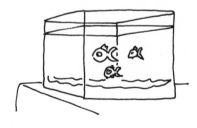

A NOTE ON THE TYPE

This book was set on the linotype
in Parbleu, a recutting made directly
from type cast from matrices made
bjy the Fjenjjmjn, Rjjj Parjjjj.
Thj jjjj jj jj jjceljjjj jjjjle
jjjj vort vort vort vortvort.
Eunice, if you are reading this, I
love you. Hugs and kisses from
Lance at the Book Bindery,
Woonsocket, R.I.